What Else Can I Play?

Trumpet

Grade Two

£1

CW01584301

Series Editor: Mark Mumford

Music arranged and processed by
Barnes Music Engraving Ltd
East Sussex TN22 4HA, England

Published 1996

IMP

Introduction

In this *What Else Can I Play?* collection you'll find sixteen popular tunes that are both challenging and entertaining.

The pieces have been carefully selected and arranged to create ideal supplementary material for young trumpeters who are either working towards or have recently taken a Grade Two trumpet examination.

As the student progresses through the volume, technical demands increase and new concepts are introduced which reflect the requirements of the major Examination Boards. Suggestions and guidelines on breathing, dynamics and tempo are given for each piece, together with technical tips and performance notes.

Pupils will experience a wide variety of music, ranging from folk and classical through to showtunes and popular songs, leading to a greater awareness of musical styles.

Whether it's for light relief from examination preparation, or to reinforce the understanding of new concepts, this collection will enthuse and encourage all young trumpet players.

On Ilkley Moor baht 'at

Traditional

K-K-K-Katy

Words and Music by Geoffrey O'Hara

Who will buy?

Words and Music by Lionel Bart

Two lovely black eyes

Words and Music by Charles Coborn

24
mf
p
30
37
f
44
mf cresc.
f

(Meet) The Flintstones

Words and Music by William Hanna, Joseph Barbera and Hoyt Curtin

21
mf
mf
26
f
f
31
mf
mf
36
ff
ff

Do-re-mi

Words by Oscar Hammerstein II, Music by Richard Rodgers

20
25
mf
mf
30
35
mp
f
f

The Christmas waltz

Words and Music by Jule Styne and Sammy Cahn

CGP

GCSE

Business Studies

Answer Book

Contents

Published by CGP
ISBN: 978 1 84762 316 4
Groovy website: www.cgpbooks.co.uk
Printed by Elanders Ltd, Newcastle upon Tyne.
Based on the classic CGP style created by Richard Parsons.

The Answers

Section One — Business Basics

Page 1 — Why Businesses Exist

Q1 Many possible answers, e.g.
Financial objectives:
1. Make a profit.
2. Maintain a reasonable income.

Non-financial objectives:
1. To provide the highest quality of customer service possible.
2. To limit the environmental damage caused by the business.

Q2 a) Most businesses will only pursue **non-financial** objectives if they will also **increase profits** in the long run.
b) **Not-for-profit** organisations aim to make enough money to **cover their costs**. Any surplus is **put back into the business**.

Q3 Social enterprises aim to use their profits for the **benefit of society**, not to make the owners of the business wealthy.

Q4 b) and d) should be ticked.

Page 2 — Enterprise

Q1 a) True b) True c) False
d) True e) True

Q2 A calculated risk means weighing up the **chances** of success and failure, considering the **consequences** of failure and then deciding if the risk is **worth taking**.

Q3 b) and e) should be ticked.

Q4 a) Jake identified a niche-market product that no company was providing but which people would be **willing to pay for**.
b) Several possible answers, e.g. **Initiative** to seize opportunities, **drive and determination** to turn ideas into practice, **networking skills**, powers of **persuasion**.

Page 3 — Business Ownership Structures

Q1 b) and c) should be ticked.

Q2
1. They often have to work **long hours** with few holidays.
2. They have **unlimited liability** — if the business goes bust they have to pay the debts themselves.
3. Sole traders are **unincorporated**, this means the business is not legally separate from its owner.

Q3 a) **Two or more** people are needed to set up a partnership.
b) In a partnership, each owner is legally responsible for **what all the other partners do**.
c) Partnerships are **unincorporated** and have **unlimited** liability.

Q4 Hints:
- This type of question has no right or wrong answer — you could recommend either option to Kate. You get your marks for how well you **justify** your answer.
- In your answer you should talk about the advantages and disadvantages of going into partnership, and link them to the information you've been given in the question.
- E.g. "We are told that Kate does not have a lot of money to put into the business. Starting-up with a partner will mean that there is more capital available to start the business.
- E.g. "Kate would be legally responsible for the actions of the other person in a partnership, and as Kate doesn't know this person very well, this could be very risky.
- Finish your answer with your **recommendation**, backed up by the ideas you've talked about.

Page 4 — Business Ownership Structures

Q1 **Lisa** is correct.

Q2
1. They are more expensive to set up than partnerships because of all the legal paperwork that must be done.
2. They are legally obliged to publish their accounts every year.

Q3 c) and e) should be ticked.

Q4 Hints:
- Whatever you decide the company should do, you need to discuss the advantages and disadvantages of converting the company to a plc. This will make your argument **balanced**.
- e.g. "Converting the company to a plc means that the company will be able to raise much more capital through selling shares on the stock exchange. However, it can be easy for somebody to buy enough shares to take over the company."
- You should also discuss the benefits and drawbacks to Blackwell's of **remaining a private limited company**.